Death before Life My Story for His Glory

Chakesha Shurn

Death Before Life: My Story for His Glory

By Chakesha Shurn

Copyright © 2017 Chakesha Shurn

Library of Congress Control Number: 2017918308

**CreateSpace Independent Publishing Platform,
North Charleston, SC**

ISBN-10: 1978277156

ISBN-13: 978-1978277151

DEDICATION

This book is dedicated to my first born child, Adriana, the joy of my life and the reason I came to worship Jesus.
Until we meet again in heaven.
I love you baby girl.

Foreword

Comfort for the Broken hearted:

My story of my greatest loss and my greatest gain!

This piece of work has been a long time coming! When I first began my journey with Christ, I received a prophecy that I would be a published author. There were never any other details, just that my story was meant to be published. I was new to Christ and was learning how to have faith in my new Savior, so this prophecy was a little far-fetched for me because I wasn't a writer. When the second and third prophecies of the same exact caliber came along, I knew it had to be of God, although I had no clue where to begin.

How was I to write a story that was ongoing? How was I to write about an event that I had not healed from? How could God expect me to relive the most hurtful time in my life and then ask me to publish it for all to see? He asked to me to relive those moments because through this process, I was being healed even more! During the process of writing, I was able to look back on the hand of God in my life, when I felt like it was only me, and see that He was there. He also asked me to write this story to inspire those like me. There are parents out there, who are in a place of despair, and need a beacon of light, just a glimmer of hope that God has His hand in the midst of all they are going through. I am here to tell you, He's there. It may not feel like it, it may not look like it, because Lord knows I didn't think He was. But, I promise you, He is there! When you wake up in the middle of the night, crying for your child, He is there. He loves you and not just an ordinary love, an unconditional, unfailing love that can never be replaced. He wants you whole and He will help you get there.

CONTENTS

ACKNOWLEDGMENTS

To my husband, Eric, the love of my life. You are the greatest reflection of how much God loves me. The way you love me, inspires me. Thank you for being patient with me. I love you.
To Mariya and Braylon, you are my everything. Mommy loves you.

Chapter 1
When the Darkness Fell

I remember my apartment being so cold and dark. It was late in the evening, on an October day in Indiana, so it had gotten dark pretty early. It was only me and my little one at home in our two bedroom apartment. I remember sitting there in the dark, with only a faint light, far off in the distance, after finding out my daughter's biological father was cheating on me. Looking back, I could literally see a darkness fall all around me. My daughter was asleep, and I was crying. I was tired of being hurt. I wondered why it was so hard for me to be loved by others? Why couldn't I love myself?

The truth of the matter was that I always had issues with self-esteem. I never felt visible or that my feelings, thoughts, or ideas mattered to anyone. So as I sat there thinking to myself, I began to cry even harder. It just felt easier to end my life. I was hurting; I didn't know how to fix the pain that I was feeling. I had no clue where to turn. I couldn't admit to my family and friends that I was broken; my pride was too strong for that. But at that very moment, God intervened on my behalf. He stepped in and showed me that He had already made a provision for my life! He had already provided a way for His glory to reign supreme in my life.

After much hesitation, trying to figure out if this was the best decision, I called my mother crying, and I said, "Ma, can I bring Adriana to you?" She asked, "why, what's wrong?" My reply was not what she expected... I said, "I can't do this anymore", "what?" She replied, and my response was, "live". And so began my journey back to life. That was the night that I was shown how much I was loved, how much I was needed, and the impact of my testimony of what was to happen next. I was able to find the strength to admit what I was going through inside, and take the first step towards Jesus and away from what Satan wanted me to do. This was the first attempt on my life-both literally and spiritually....

After breaking down over the phone with my mom, I gathered a bag of clothes for Adriana and I drove over to her house. When I arrived, she was waiting in the doorway, in her coat, ready to go. She told me to get in the passenger seat and she drove me to the emergency room at the hospital. After the doctor examined me and asked me a series of questions, one of the stipulations of my release was to enter an outpatient psychiatric program along with a promise to not harm myself. Although I was reluctant, I agreed, and they voluntarily released me. That night I ended up staying at my mother's house. This was new to her; it was new to me! I had never been so depressed that I wanted to take my own life. I think my mother was terrified for my well being as well as the welfare of my baby girl. However, the incidence of depression in our family was one that I never knew was so prevalent. Looking back, I understand why my mother behaved the way she did at times. She too was depressed, but I couldn't recognize it until it fell upon me.

Although I was still a little hesitant, I began the outpatient program the next day. I remember the day vividly because it started early. It was a bright and sunny day, a stark contrast to the night I had experienced previously. I couldn't believe I was in a room with people who had similar thoughts as I did. Individuals who had felt the weight of life and had finally cracked under the pressure, just as I had. But I felt comfortable telling my story to everyone there. We shared, laughed, and cried together; we embraced each other like we had known each other for years. We were able to bond over our emotional pain. I was able to work through some of my thoughts and was ultimately placed on an anti-depressant to help me cope with the feelings I was having.

It was a great stabilizer. Who knew I would need psychiatric care and the medication at a few more stages in my life.

****

It's in the times of confusion and heartache, the time when you need the light, that's the time darkness shows up. It's in those times that the light is furthest away. It seems like the light is the hardest to reach. No matter how hard you try, the closer you get, the further away the light appears. But it's an illusion, because the light is always there, up close and personal.

Chapter 2
How It Began

Eric and I had known each other for many years. I met him in eighth grade at a birthday party for my cousin, and we dated, as much as an eighth grader can date someone, but he was my first love. He wasn't like the rest. He was gentle, kind, patient, and he loved me. That was enough for me. We separated during high school and went about our separate lives. Shortly into adulthood, I met and started dating Adriana's biological father, and soon after got pregnant with Adriana. By the time she was born, our relationship was very rocky. During my pregnancy, I ran into

Eric, and we rekindled our friendship. He was going through a divorce, that was finalized the end of 2004, and I had more than enough on my plate at the time. He would encourage me, lighten my mood, as I was still dealing with the depression and he was just all around a great friend, never overstepping boundaries.

My pregnancy proved to be difficult because from the day I found out I was pregnant, I couldn't keep any food down. It was so bad that I was unable to keep water down. I was on bed rest from the time I received the news of my pregnancy until I was about five and a half months along. The doctors confirmed that I had a healthy, viable pregnancy, however I was also suffering from severe hyperemesis which caused me to lose at total of 30 lbs. throughout the course of my pregnancy. I was placed on a Reglan pump in an attempt to curb my nausea and vomiting. Ultimately, I felt like I was lying in my apartment dying. I had this little person growing inside me that was taking every last nutrient from me. I wanted to be

excited about being pregnant. I wanted to feel the "pregnancy glow" that so many women acquire while with child. Unfortunately, I felt horrible. The doctors couldn't help me and I basically had to stick it out until my little one made her appearance into this world. I couldn't wait for her to get here!
My little bundle of joy, my princess was born on April 19, 2004 at 2:01 am. I named her Adriana Sierra.

The night prior, I had begun leaking amniotic fluid, so the doctor decided to induce me. Adriana didn't make her debut until quite sometime later, 12 hours later to be exact. Nonetheless, when she did, I felt complete. I was required to have her by cesarean section because after 11 hours of labor and no progression, my little one was in distress. The doctors rushed me into emergency surgery and at 2:01 am, they laid a sweet, beautiful baby girl on my chest, after cleaning her up of course.

During the cesarean section, I was stricken with a uterine infection so I was immediately put on intravenous antibiotics, that ultimately prolonged my recovery process. By the time I came out of recovery, and Adriana and I were reunited, the sun was shining brightly, an indication of light being brought into my life! She was beautiful! She had ten fingers and ten toes; she started off with these beautiful grey eyes and this beautiful jet black, bone straight hair that wrapped around her tiny little head. She was so small; she only weighed 6lbs even. This was the happiest day of my life! She was so adorable even the nurses couldn't resist putting little bows on her hair every time she would visit the nursery!

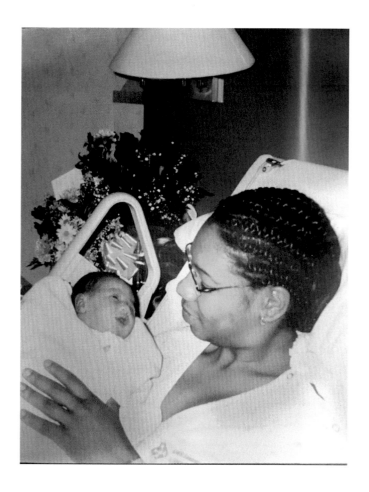

Throughout my pregnancy and after Adriana was born my relationship with her biological father was extremely rocky. We weren't living together and I felt disconnected from him. Shortly after she was born, I felt I needed to get away from life as I knew it, to clear my mind. When Eric offered for Adriana and I to come visit with him at his apartment in Ohio, I struggled with whether or not I should go. I knew how it would appear from the outside looking in, but ultimately, I needed a break, so I decided to go. Eric was a complete gentleman. He slept on the couch while giving Adriana and I the bed. Adriana was only six weeks old at the time, but it was great to get away and just relax. Adriana was about a year and a half old when her biological father and I broke it off. We wanted different things out of life, and there were several circumstances, including the one that led to our separation, which were unacceptable for me to deal with.

During this time, Eric and I kept in contact; I stayed busy working as an Insurance Agent and taking care of Adriana. In addition, I continued to work on myself through my outpatient program. Around the summer of 2005, Eric had attempted to propose to me, but since I was in a difficult place mentally, I assumed he was joking. When he came to visit me in the winter of 2005 with a ring, and asked me to marry him for the second time, I knew it was real and finally said yes. He said he knew I was the one. He had known since we met back in eighth grade. Eric was stationed in Ohio while Adriana and I were residing in Indiana. After he proposed, Adriana and I started our new year, in a new state.

In April of 2006, we celebrated Adriana's second birthday. Nothing fancy, because we were in a new city and didn't know anyone with little children. The day was actually very laid back. We got her a little cupcake and sang happy birthday to her. She smiled and was extremely excited. She was loved, and for Adriana, that was all she needed!

It was May 2006, and our wedding day was fast approaching. Eric and I were overjoyed to be able to share our love in front of our loved ones. We were excited about the new life we were beginning together! Even though Adriana was from a previous relationship, that meant nothing to Eric... he loved her like his own child, and she loved him. She had gotten so attached to him that she began calling him "Daddy" all on her own. He came home from work one day, and she ran to greet him as she always did, but this time she yelled, "Hi Daddy!" Her bond with her daddy was amazing! She loved to ride in daddy's car. For some reason, daddy's car was cooler than mommy's car. Daddy would take her to McDonald's and get her favorite foods (chicken nuggets and French fries). She would dance and sing for hours as Eric would play music on the computer, then she would cuddle up in his lap and suck her two fingers. That was her comfort, her security blanket. Before we got to Ohio, Eric already had a large fish tank, and when we moved in, he bought fish that Adriana got extremely attached to. She loved to sit and watch her "fishies", as she called them. Whenever we would leave the house, she had to say goodbye to her fishies. "Bye fishies, see you later," her little voice was melodic to my ears.

Our wedding day had finally arrived. Everything was perfect; and went off without a hitch! Adriana was one of our two flower girls. She was the cutest little thing! She was supposed to be pulled in a wagon by our older flower girl down the aisle, but instead, she grabbed the handle and took off running down the aisle alone! The entire audience erupted in laughter! She definitely made our wedding day memorable!

Chakesha Shurn

After the wedding, Eric and I went on our honeymoon to Las Vegas and Adriana stayed with my dad for the five days we were gone. One day I called to talk to her, and she and Pawpaw were on the balcony having breakfast because it was such a beautiful day. As people walked past, she yelled "Hi," to them and smiled. She was just like that, loving and friendly. When we returned, our lives went back to normal. We lived in Columbus, Ohio where Eric was stationed in the military. I was fortunate to be able to transfer my job to be with him, and everything was going smoothly until the last week in May when Adriana became ill. I wasn't worried because I had taken care of her numerous times before with common colds and the occasional slight fever, and this time wasn't any different, so I thought.

We immediately knew something was wrong because she didn't want to eat her favorite, chicken nuggets and

French fries. I went about my day to day, making sure she was comfortable. She would lay around the apartment and I would try to get her to drink fluids since she wouldn't eat. I was sure this was just a bug that would pass and we would get back to our lives. We first noticed Adriana was feeling ill on Sunday of that week. I took her to see her doctor for the first time on Monday because I had no clue why she had a fever. The doctor and I were on the same page, she thought it was a virus as well. She told me to wait a few days to see if the fever would break by alternating ibuprofen and acetaminophen. By Thursday, Adriana still had the fever, but she also could not walk and needed to be carried. I took her in Thursday morning and, the doctor recommended I take her to the children's hospital, so I did.

I'm still not alarmed at this time because I never thought that anything bad would ever happen. At the children's hospital, they performed a spinal tap because by now, I had to carry her everywhere, and she was very lethargic on top of not eating. The nurse came back and said there were white blood cells in her spinal fluid which indicated an infection and they wanted to keep her overnight. Adriana attended daycare because both her dad and I were working, however, this particular week I stayed home with my sick child. It was my job to make sure my baby girl got well, after all, I was her mommy and that's what mommy's do. Now at this point, I'm still not worried and looking back, it had to have been the peace of God because I was calm and oblivious to what was about to take place. The doctors admitted her to the hospital on Thursday evening. Eric still had to work, but I was not leaving my baby's side, so the next day, which was Friday, I asked my husband to bring Adriana a change of clothes when he got off of work so she could have something clean to wear when she was to be released. That was the night when they intubated her and moved her to the Pediatric Intensive Care Unit (PICU)....

Even in the state that she was in, I still wasn't worried. I spoke to my parents, and they didn't like the sound of it, so they drove to Columbus along with my sister. When they arrived, they talked to Adriana and stayed at the hospital as long as visiting hours would allow them, then they all went back to our apartment. I still was not leaving my peanut's side (as I called her)...

Chapter 3
June 3, 2006

Then it happened...early Saturday morning the monitors started going crazy, and the medical team rushed in. My husband and I were in a panic, as any parents would be, and we stood there holding each other as they revived our two-year-old daughter three separate times. Then all of a sudden, the doctor looked over at us and said, "I'm sorry, there's nothing else we can do"........................ My legs gave out, and I fell to the floor. I burst into sobs. I could not believe what I was hearing! How can my healthy, bright, beautiful baby girl be gone? How could this little person that I loved so much be taken from me? I believed the doctors when they said she would be okay. I thought that she was going home with me, but now I was hearing she was gone??? How could this be? I screamed and yelled. I cried for my baby girl, but she was gone. Making the calls to my parents and to her biological father were hard. How does one deliver such news?

The nurses unhooked her from all the monitors and tubes, and by this time, my family was back in the hospital room along with a few close friends. We were all in total shock and disbelief. They allowed me to hold her and say my last goodbyes. As I held and kissed her, my mind began playing tricks on me because I could have sworn I could see her chest moving up and down. I yelled for the nurse and insisted that she check her. But it was my mind...playing a cruel, yet hopeful trick. The progression of this illness lasted only a week. She began feeling ill on Sunday and by Saturday morning, my child was gone. Adriana passed away in the early morning hours of June 3rd, 2006 from Meningoencephalitis with complications from pneumonia.

Chapter 4
The Walk of Pain

Leaving the hospital without my child was the weirdest, most painful act I have ever experienced. I was wheeled out in a wheel chair because my legs had given out numerous times. As we walked down the quiet hallways, with her stuffed dinosaur and diaper bag full of fresh clothes that Eric had brought for her to leave the hospital in, I died on the inside. I was crushed. This little girl was my world. I woke up to her and went to sleep with her. Going back to an empty house, was heartbreaking because so many memories had just occurred. Simple things like getting in the car and not having to strap her in the car seat tore my heart apart! No pain compares to losing a child. Period.

I had died on the inside; I couldn't breathe a breath of life, I felt like I was suffocating at all times. I was completely numb and could only hear the voice of the enemy telling me it was ok to end it... It was ok to throw in the towel because it was my child, she was my everything.

When I look back, I can see (with my spiritual eyes) how many times God tried to get my attention. I can see where I went wrong, what my sins were, and later, as my healing process began and I began to walk more aligned with God, how my story reminded me of King David's story in the bible. God was gracious enough to provide me with everything I needed before this tragedy. I had a great job and was able to provide for my daughter without assistance. I was independent, living life on my terms, not paying attention to the subtle signs sent by God heeding warning.

But this was not God's doing. Yes, God took her because He couldn't allow her to be anything less than the perfection she was. Would I have been able to handle having a brain dead child without God? Could I handle taking care of a disabled child when I had already been provided with just enough to take care of my healthy one? God showed me, and Adriana, His grace, and His mercy. I had to hit rock bottom to see that He was the Rock at the bottom. Some would say that this statement is inappropriate to say, however, I truly believe that her loss of life saved my life!

Chapter 5
June 10, 2006

To follow the worst day of my life, on June 10, a week after Adriana's passing, was her funeral, my last goodbye to my baby girl. I remember being nervous, and not really feeling I was strong enough to see my baby girl lying in a casket. There's no way to really prepare yourself to see your child in a casket. The preparation of her body, such as her clothes and ensuring her hair was picture perfect was done by my mother and sisters because I was not strong enough to do it.

Naturally, I was anxious because

didn't know what to expect when I saw her. Of course, I knew she would be gorgeous because she was my princess. I think I was nervous about how she would look. Would I be able to see where her autopsy was performed? Would she look like herself? Would I recognize her beautiful face or would she look like someone I didn't know? All of this constantly ran through my mind.

The limo came to pick my husband and I up. It was the longest ride across our small town ever. I was a ball of emotions; I was sad, mad, and nervous all at once. When we pulled up at the church, my heart stopped. I didn't want to go in but I knew I had to. I hesitated as I was escorted out of the limo on my husband's arm. I walked in with my husband and my father on either side of me. This was more of a precaution, just in case my legs gave out again, but I also needed both of their emotional strength during this time. I felt like I was in the twilight zone, it was like I had tunnel vision to her casket. I knew there were people, my loved ones, flowers and a more substantial surrounding; however, all I saw was her casket. I walked up to the casket slowly, and I remember standing there just staring at her. She looked like a life-size baby doll, complete with two pigtails. My baby doll that had left me.

■■ ı

Two months after Adriana passed away, I found out I was six weeks pregnant! Eric and I were excited, but it was also a little bittersweet. It was a breath of fresh air until it wasn't. I began to notice bleeding. Unfortunately, I knew what that meant or could mean, so we headed to the emergency room. We sat in the waiting room for hours before we were called back. I remember feeling this was an urgent matter and wanting the hospital staff to think so too. It turns out, if I was already in the process of miscarrying, there was nothing that could be done. That's why it wasn't urgent for them.

When we got in a room, we still waited for what seemed like forever for the doctor to come in. When he finally arrived, he was rude and very dismissive. He had no compassion for what my husband and I were going through. They performed an ultrasound and found an empty womb. My body had already expelled the baby. The way the doctor announced it to us was just horrid. He then walked out and left us in this cold room with the lingering of his icy response. We ended up leaving before they officially discharged us because he never came back in the room to tell us what we should do next. This hurt. It was another jab in an already open and bleeding wound.

Those first couple months without Adriana were unbearable. We lived in a two bedroom apartment, therefore, her room was right next door to ours. It took a year for me to be able to go into her room. Eric cleaned it out for me. I couldn't stand to see her bed and her toys; it just broke my heart all over again. After Adriana passed, I could not bring myself to sleep in our bedroom either since it was so close to her room. I slept on the couch and Eric slept on the floor right beside me. He wouldn't leave my side. There were numerous nights where I would wake up screaming and crying or thinking I heard my peanut crying and Eric would turn on soothing music and hold me close, rocking me back to sleep as if I were a baby. Eric was an amazing support during this rough moment for me.

During this time, while still living in Ohio, is when depression set in stronger than ever and Eric was afraid to leave me home alone while he worked. I had fallen so deep into depression that I had begun cutting and harming myself. I didn't want to live. Living after this loss and with this pain was agonizing. Eric ended up hiding any and everything that could be used as a weapon to harm myself, including all the knives in the kitchen.

Eric worked at a recruiting station that also distributed testing for military applicants, so he spoke to his commanding officer and explained the situation to him. The chain of command was on board with allowing me to come to work with my husband and stay

until he was off of work. This was a
lifesaver, literally! I hadn't returned to
work, because emotionally, I was
incapable. I was a wreck most days.
Staying at home alone was not an
option since I had attempted suicide, so
for Eric's command to be willing to
accommodate us in this extreme
situation, I am forever grateful.

■■■

    Shortly after the miscarriage, we
found out we were pregnant with
Mariya. I was excited, yet nervous and
scared all at the same time. I had
already endured a miscarriage
immediately after losing my first born
child and here I was pregnant again. I
was a ball of emotions; I was dealing
with grief times 2. I had so many
questions swirling around in my mind
all at once. Was I going to be able to
carry this baby to term? Was God trying
to replace the child I already had? How
was I going to love this child the way I
loved Adriana? All of these emotions
swirled on the inside of me, so I began
to detach myself from being excited.
Even after Mariya was born, I found

that my interactions with her were from beyond a wall. I didn't want to get too attached to her, just in case something bad happened to her.

After giving birth to our beautiful baby girl, Mariya Tanee in May of 2007, I requested that my doctor perform a tubal ligation. In my mind, I was done with having children, but by the grace of God, my doctor said he couldn't honor my request knowing what I had gone through so recently.

I had stood in the room and watched my daughter flat line! I was scared that I would have to go through the same thing once again. I was emotionally drained. Then, I myself had flat lined; I'd been resuscitated, by my own strength, for a while, then would flat line again... I flatlined for the last time in 2008, a year after I had my second child Mariya. 2008 was the year I chose to live and not die! I had to live, there was another little life depending on me. I decided to seek the help of the Great Helper because only He could keep me from death, naturally and spiritually!

I always wanted to know why me??? Why would I be chosen to endure such heartache? There is no more profound sorrow than for a parent to have to bury their child. There's no more profound pain, nothing compares! Nothing! You know, I used to always look at others and wonder why they were going through the things they were and I would still think, "nothing like that would ever happen to me", why did I believe that??? I don't know... maybe subconsciously I felt invincible or that I wasn't important enough to where significant events would befall me. Maybe I felt that only people who were relevant and important enough to have a light shone on their life, went through things like this. Well, I guess I was one of the people I never imagined to be. I suppose I was to be one of those "important" people who were to be made an example of. I almost didn't pass the test, I almost gave up and took the easy way out. I almost believed the lies whispered in my ear...

The tears roll down my cheek as I

write this, all I know was that my husband was by my side when all the smoke cleared. And while everyone else went back to their happy lives, and I was left with pieces...he was there! What I didn't realize was that God was there also, standing by my side waiting for me to reach out to Him, to acknowledge Him, to seek His face, to ask Him to heal me. I was oblivious to this fact, and therefore my husband had to continue watching me suffer.

It is a choice I had made to exist in a "dead" state. Many don't know that they have a choice whether or not they die. Once we find Christ, He can give us the life we deserve through Him.

Chapter 6
Who Was Adriana?

When I speak about my daughter, I smile... I smile because I know where she is without a shadow of a doubt. I get emotional when I give my testimony in front of large crowds because I can feel their anguish over my loss. I can sense their emotion for myself and my husband and our little peanut. But when I hear her name, it brings me joy because I know that she still lives on in the hearts of others, just as she does in mine. I know she looks down on my and her dad's every move because that's how much she loves us! Her death doesn't control my life any longer. Losing her was the single most tragic event of my life, but it does not consume me as it once did. I thank God for peace, comfort, and healing, because without Him I would still be in a hell of the replay after replay in my mind of her death! I thank God for taking away most of the bad memories and leaving the good! Only an extraordinary God would do that!

Adriana was like a little light for me. A small light, but an extremely bright light! She was always smiling! She had a smile that would make you beam just by looking at her. Her brother actually has that same smile now and reminds me daily of her light. She loved her mommy. She was my little twin. She was barely ever out of my sight, however, the rare times that she was, she was always so happy to see me when I returned. She was a friendly little person which is a trait her baby brother has as well. She loved to dance. Any ounce of music would send her into a fit of dancing, which is a fantastic attribute of both her brother and sister!

They dance constantly!

Adriana loved Sponge Bob and Dora the Explorer, but her absolute favorite was Blue's Clues! She had a 19" television that was all hers, that had a VHS player attached, and she would rewind her Blue's Clues video and watch it at least 15 times a day, all on her own. Her level of intelligence was remarkable. She was advanced in so many areas. I honestly believe that Ms. Adriana was my guardian angel. And she felt that once my husband and I got married, I was in good hands and it was ok for her to go. We got married in May, and she left me physically in June.

Chapter 7
How HE Used Me

In the midst of all of my heartache and pain, while I was going through the stages of my healing through Christ, the Master Restorer saw fit to use me to bring glory to Him.

After Adriana's death, and our next military move, that suicidal spirit came back stronger than ever. My suicidal attempts and thoughts were overwhelming to the point where my husband was still afraid to leave me home alone while he went to work. We were in Virginia by now, further away from all family due to military orders and I had just given birth to our daughter Mariya.

Even though our baby girl Mariya was a bright light in the middle of such darkness, I couldn't shake the gloom that towered over me. I felt stuck in a deep, dark pit and I didn't know how to get out. My husband took a chance and talked to his supervising Senior Chief, who became like family to us, and he pointed us in the direction of a church that would introduce us to our God, who would change our lives forever. In the interim, I sought an appointment with a therapist in our new state who had placed me on anti-depressants, and in the meantime, we began some much-needed grief counseling and also began to attend church. Even in the midst of all of my trials, my healing began. God had a greater purpose for me. He began to use me in a mighty way. I started to learn so many things about my Heavenly Father- who He was, how much He loved me, and who I was. At this church, a prophetic word was spoken over me, (one of many) a word that changed my life. The gift of healing was activated on the inside of me, and

God began a great work in and through me. In the New Testament, the book of Mark 16:15-18, NIV, Jesus said to His disciples, "Go into all the world and preach the gospel to all creation. Whoever believes and is baptized will be saved, but whoever does not believe will be condemned. And these signs will accompany those who believe: In my name they will drive out demons; they will speak in new tongues; they will pick up snakes with their hands; and when they drink deadly poison, it will not hurt them at all; they will place their hands on sick people, and they will get well." And that is exactly what happened. God began to use me to bring healing to people, through the laying of hands. This is something that is used in churches when a great healing is needed. One that only God can perform.

While at this church, my husband and I made the decision to be baptized together. This decision symbolized us leaving behind the death that had overtaken us and stepping into a full life in Christ (Jn. 10:10). I began to pray effectively, and God would turn things around (Jas. 5:16). I was submitted to His purpose in my life, and He was transforming me right before my very eyes. I was now beginning to see the world on a spiritual level, and everything changed. I was a new creature now. My husband and I noticed a drastic lifestyle change. Our desires were different than they had been before. We no longer wanted to party and drink. We no longer wanted to curse and use foul language as we had for so long. We were being cleansed by the Holy Spirit and by the Word of God.

After some healing had taken place and God had begun to restore me, I was adamant about having another baby, despite my horrid experience with sickness during my previous pregnancies. I was convinced I heard the voice of God letting me know that this pregnancy would be different. He was right, it was different, however not in the manner I expected. This was my worst pregnancy yet, and doctors predicted I might never be able to walk again because of the amount of nerve damage I had experienced. By the year 2010, a month before Mariya turned three years old, our little Braylon Alexander was born. Even after our great losses and challenged faith, God blessed us with more little ones to love.

After staying home with Braylon for about a year, I wanted to go back to work. Eric was on board with me staying home, however, I wanted more adult interaction. I got a job at an insurance agency because I had been a licensed insurance agent since before I got pregnant with Adriana. It was a small office that had an abundance of clients. I had a small little office in the back. The clientele that would come in were from all walks of life. It was interesting how God would set up these "meet and greets" for my clients and I to commune in His presence. The set-up of the agency was one that didn't require clients to speak with an agent for simple things like making a payment, however, clients would request to speak to me because they knew that the Lord held a word for them through me.

During this season of my life, God would use me to bring words of encouragement to everyone who stepped into my office. I found myself praying for and with people through their various situations, disappointments and hardships. I had a co-worker who had tried for 10 whole years to get pregnant with no luck. She asked me to pray for her and trust God with her that her womb would be fruitful. God is faithful because she reported she was pregnant within the next month! This was after 10 barren years and multiple doctors advising her that she would never get pregnant!

Testimonies would pour in daily on how God had answered prayers prayed in my office. Not only did I pray for others, they would pray for me as well. It didn't matter the day, whether good or bad, the presence of the Lord was in the building. God allowed me to see and feel the impact that my prayers had on those around me.

****

I believe 2013 was the year when I really stepped out and began to develop my own connection and relationship with God... not that I didn't have one before, but admittedly it was more influenced by religion, not a relationship. So once my connection with Christ was more developed, I began to understand and walk in the things of God! For instance, around this time we stopped celebrating Halloween. We realized that in this case, it was more important for us to celebrate light; for us, it was a choice we made to honor God (Deut. 5:33). Some things that we consider fun, do not always honor and acknowledge God, it's just that plain and simple. When we choose to walk with Christ, we give up our will for His, so some of the things we find fun are no longer in His will for us! Does it suck?? Yes, but it also prevents us from dying in sin! And it sometimes comes down to being in His will or having fun. Choose this day who you will follow. I'm not saying that it will

always be a choice, and we can never
have fun, but we should hate what the
Father hates and love what the Father
loves (Rom. 12:9). When you know
better, you do better... so we should
know that although He rains on the just
as well as the unjust (Matt. 5:45), He
can't bless us with what He wants to, if
we're not willing to let go of some
things.

In 1st Samuel, Chapter 30:8, it is
shown that God will touch the heart of
Kings, as He did King David, resulting
in prayer and intercession. My God!!!
God showed me in this particular
instance, that my prayers were
important and needed. On Jan 8, 2013,
I had a dream while I was sleeping, a
vision of sorts, eerily similar to the
situation in Cleveland, Ohio with the
man holding three girls in bondage. In
my dream, I saw two tall cylinder blocks
that were about six feet tall. Above the
blocks were chains with cuffs on the
ends, hanging from the ceiling. In each
cylinder was a girl with her arms
chained inside the cuffs. Above the
cylinder blocks were the words "Ohio

Bondage". My dream was completely silent, but those words were loud. I began to pray for these women who I didn't know existed. I prayed nightly until I felt a godly peace. Four months later, in early May of 2013, those girls were found and released! The girls had been chained up inside their abductor's residence for years.

When the story was released on the news, one of the young women described similar conditions to what I saw in my dream. I feel like those girls had to be praying, they were praying, so was I and probably many others who God gave this assignment to. As believers of God, it may be placed on our hearts to pray for someone we do not know much about. In 1 Chron. 21:16, God had placed a plague on the people of Israel and as the King, David was led to pray on behalf the people of Jerusalem. Just as God gave the assignment of prayer to King David, who had faith enough to pray, He gave me the assignment to pray for these young women, even though I didn't know what I was praying for!!!

****

This holiday season is particularly challenging, but I am determined to hang on to my healing! I have had my peanut on my mind like crazy! I miss her so much... I can't even describe the aching my heart feels without her. I'm up nights thinking about her and daydreaming during the day thinking of her. I can truly say that I am standing on Gods word that I will see her again and there will be no more pain, hurt or suffering (Rev. 21:4).

Although I miss her so much, I still feel peaceful... It's a bit strange, but I know that it's the work of the Father... keeping me! I can't help but want to see her little eyes, kiss her sweet face and squeeze her tight! I could have easily been a Scrooge this year for the holidays, but I chose to bring cheer. How do you bring joy when you're sad??? You can do something for someone else, something they couldn't do for themselves.

I'm learning that if you do your part, God will do His. And trust is when you go with the flow, and KNOW that He'll do His! It's not your business, nor responsibility to know what His role is. I never knew why my favorite scripture was Proverbs 3:5-6,"Trust in The Lord with all your heart and lean not to your own understanding, in all your ways acknowledge Him and He will direct your paths" until tonight (November 14, 2013, 12:41 am)! And when that truth settled in my heart, a burden lifted off my shoulders!

Chapter 8
How This Changed My Relationships

A loss of this caliber could have quickly ended my marriage. We got married May of 2006, and she passed in June! So from the beginning, our marriage, our commitment, and our love was truly tested for its strength. Love is a verb, an action word, and when you say that you love someone, it not only needs to come from your mouth but also from your actions. My husband could have easily left me after this happened. After all, he wasn't her biological father and therefore was not obligated to stay in any way. And in all honesty, it was a long road that neither one of us expected to endure. How do you show someone that you love them? Stand right next to them when it's easier to walk out on them, be there to pick up the pieces as they fall and help them put the puzzle back together. Never allow your frustration with the process of healing to slow, or undermine the work that has been done. Lastly, do all that you can to support the person you love!

Throughout the entirety of this ordeal, Eric was there with open arms. He comforted me, he loved me, and he never left me to face it alone. That spoke volumes to me, so when I had the chance, I wanted to make sure he knew how grateful I was for him. In November of 2011, I was able to show him the same love he taught me. A few months prior, I had a nagging feeling that something terrible was about to happen. I prayed and prayed about it. Then the Holy Spirit placed on my heart a feeling there was something wrong with Eric. Although I could not pinpoint what it was, it just kept nagging at me.

When Eric would get ready for work, he would use the guest bathroom, because it was so early, he didn't want to wake me. Well, as Eric was getting ready for work early one morning, he blacked out, fell backwards into the wall and hit the floor leaving a massive hole in the bathroom wall. Meanwhile, I thought I heard a thud, but did not get up to check to see what it was. Shortly after I heard the thud sound, my cell phone rang, it was Eric telling me to come into the guest bathroom. I immediately jumped out of bed and ran to the bathroom, but when I tried to open the door, it seemed to be stuck, as if something was in front of it. After some pushing, I finally got it open, and there he was lying on the floor delirious and sweating profusely.

Due to the amount of blood he had already lost, he was too weak to walk and therefore I had to assist him in sliding down the stairs. He didn't want an ambulance, so I did what I had to do. I put his arm around my neck and helped him get up. I put him in my car and drive him to the nearest hospital.

After I got him to the hospital, and a few tests had been run, we were told that he had experienced upper gastrointestinal bleeding, and his red blood cell count was severely low, almost to the point of needing a blood transfusion. He was then transferred to the military hospital by ambulance and placed in the Intensive Care Unit for four days. I sat by his side; I prayed, cried and pleaded with the Lord on his behalf. I never left his side, just as he never left mine.

There would be three more incidents where he was hospitalized and/or required surgery (a complete Achilles' tendon rupture, and two major back surgeries). Although these events were stressful, it was my pleasure to care for, and cater to my husband.

One thing I have learned is to always be thankful for your journey and the pathways that God has carved out for you. These trials and triumphs are tailor made for you individually. You never know what someone else's path entails. You are unaware of their struggles behind closed doors, their pain in the darkness, and their attacks whcn alone.

Chapter 9
Lessons Learned During Resuscitation

One Christmas after Adriana passed away, my dad gave myself and my sisters a book to read. Now at first glance, I thought it might be boring, but it turned out to be a lifesaver! It completely changed my perspective on who, what, when, where, and why my God was. It made me view God on a different level. He gave me the book when the healing stage had already begun in my life, so I was accepting of the new perspective and appreciative the freshness it brought to my life. This book not only changed my outlook on

my life as I perceived it, but it turned
my praise, worship and adoration
towards the God I had come to know. I
believe, in some ways that writing this
book facilitated a faster route to my
healing process! Healing became
inevitable in my eyes when just prior, I
could barely see it on the horizon. I
think what I knew, but failed to grasp
fully is that God is a loving God! He is
not a God of war, discord, or hate, but a
God of love. He had so much more love
for my Adriana than I could ever give
her... and He loved her enough to not
allow her to be anything less than the
perfection He created! Don't get me
wrong here, every creature God brings
into being- no matter the color, stature,
intellect...are all His precious creations,
but I had to trust that my pain was for
a greater good in my life.

   As I type, I am reminded of the
biblical story of Abraham and Ishmael,
and how Abraham trusted God so much
to the point that He was willing to send
his own son(Ishmael), away for a higher
purpose. An angel spoke to Haggar,
who was pregnant with Ishmael, and

said, "You are now pregnant and will give birth to a son. You shall name him Ishmael (which means 'God hears'), for the Lord, has heard of your misery" (Gen. 16:11). Whatever that reason was for Abraham to send his son Ishmael away, it wasn't Abraham's responsibility to know what God's plan was; it was his responsibility to obey and allow God to do His part. I feel like I had an Abraham-like experience without me knowing.

I was in such a horrid place in my life, that I was oblivious to Gods voice and instruction. I knew nothing of the required obedience and faith it would take to possibly "keep" my daughter here with me! I only knew the power of self...and self, has no power at all. It occurred to me a few months ago that I had the ability, through the Holy Spirit, to heal Adriana back in 2006. I had the healing power of the Holy Spirit inside of me, but I had not been adequately introduced to the Holy Spirit and did not know how to call on said power! Oh, but now my faith will move mountains, and I can testify to the goodness of God.

Perhaps it is not what others would consider good, but it is my own personal account of His goodness!

Chapter 10
Tragedy to Triumph

Many of the people I speak to about the tragedy of losing a child, are those who are in the early stages of grief. Seeing past the hurt, heartbreak, and feelings of abandonment are difficult during the beginning stages. You wonder, where was God during all of this? Why would He allow my child to die, if He is all-powerful and controls everything? My sister actually struggled with these feelings much longer than I did. I knew I was healed from this pain controlling my life when I was able to give my testimony for the very first time in front of a large crowd at church, without tears, fear, or grief. I felt like I could breathe! I had, at one point, gone entirely off a spiritual cliff and was completely shattered to pieces...but my God picked up every piece, big and small, significant and insignificant and put them back together. He carefully pieced each broken part of my life back together-sanded, painted, and polished every piece and made me look and feel brand new. The carpenter made me whole for the first time. Because we are born with a sinful nature, I was at comfortable living a broken life, yet didn't know the fullness that was available to me through Jesus Christ! It was through the healing of my brokenness, that I began to experience LIFE! He showed me a death that is sin, loss, and despair, then revived me with His fresh oil, and His bright red blood! He gave me life!

When God does the healing, you will have a visible scar for others to see, but you are no longer bleeding internally. Your internal bleeding has stopped- and your body, mind, and spirit are able to function the way God designed them to work. While you are bleeding, your insides are being contaminated, and major organs begin to fail. Your heart has stopped beating, your liver and pancreas are not filtering the waste, and everything is contaminated! Oh, but when God stops the bleeding, when He heals your soul and your spirit, the bleeding stops... your lungs are clear, your heart beats, and the waste is cleaned out. When God does it, you can guarantee it will be done right!

There are only a few things in life that we can control, so when we do what's right with those few things, God will put the rest into place!

At one point I was so contaminated, I had so much vile waste inside of me that the enemy convinced me that I would be better off if I just took my life. So that's what I tried to do! I had lost my everything, so there was no reason for me to live right??? Wrong!!! God had a plan for my life! He had a mighty plan that I had to live long enough to see come to fruition! So He intervened and

set me up for the journey of my life...
back to life! God reminded me that this
fight is fixed in my favor!

Not only did God heal me from the
pain and anguish of losing my first born
daughter, but He also healed me from
depression, suicidal thoughts and
miscarriage! He taught me that I was
worth so much more than what the
enemy had led me to believe. He
nurtured me and showed me the
pedestal that He sees me sitting on, and
gave me the strength to see myself there
as well!

The things that I felt were fun and
addicting and oh so worldly were the
very things that were killing me. They
were the very things that kept me from
hearing the voice of God. He was calling
my name for so long, but I was so busy
doing what I wanted to do, not caring
nor realizing my ultimate duty here on
earth...to bring the Gospel of Jesus
Christ to the lost and to be an
inspiration to those who needed it. I
couldn't hear and comply because I was
one of those lost ones. I hadn't heard

the Gospel; I hadn't heard the good news of Jesus Christ. I was lost, but as He began to revive me, the lessons of life began to roll in. My eyes were opened, and I could see the world for what it was. He saved me from me.

He saved me from believing the lies the enemy had told me, and it took some years, but He restored me. I didn't know Christ then but through this pain, the ultimate love was found. And though I miss her, I am grateful that she was able to help me to reconcile with the most significant love of all! Through my salvation, through the love of Christ, He has healed a wound that was raw and gaping for so long. Little by little, as I was ready, He gave me more and more strength. He gave me the clarity to be able to understand His grace. I have learned to snuggle up to Jesus not only through life's trials, but always because only a Savior who truly loves me unconditionally, with flaws and all, would snatch me from a situation where I almost took my own life. Only a loving Savior would build me back upon a sturdy foundation so that I would be able to withstand anything that came my way. Jesus gave me life after death.

I learned who I was and how much strength God had given me when He created me. He didn't create me to break, yet when I didn't know the love of my Father, I crumbled under pressure. God did not create us to be weakened by life's circumstances, nor did He create us to be the victim constantly. He created us to overcome. God once told me that I was created for Him to love...for Him to love??? Before, I couldn't fathom how little ol' me could be so important to such a great big God, but through my healing, He showed me how.

Amidst all the chaos of pain, healing, and recovery, I began to learn who I was. Or should I say, who God had called me to be. I knew He had called me to be a mother and a wife, but I didn't know that my identity also included an anointing so great, that there was no wonder why the enemy wanted me dead. See, the tragedy of losing my daughter brought so much pain, but it also allowed me to tap into the power that God had placed within me. I often hear my mother tell the story of her being pregnant with me. She knew she was pregnant, but for months on end, the doctors told her she wasn't. They would send her home, and she would cry, but she always came back and told them to check again. Finally, they saw what she had already known. I was strong then, and I began to learn how strong I was later in life as well. There's a saying "God gives His toughest battles to his strongest children". That's how God showed me who I was, and how strong I was. He allowed a trial that the enemy thought would kill me, but God knew I would overcome. I would deny for months, even years that the activated anointing to heal, the power God had placed within me wasn't real, or that I didn't have it. That was until the day God showed me His power through me, and I could no longer deny it.

Chapter 11
Who Am I?

The loss of my precious baby girl was the beginning of a process to becoming who I am today. In 2015, I received a word of confirmation on my calling from God through a close friend and it gave me life all over again. The word said, "the world knows you as Chakesha Shurn, names given and obtained through birth and marriage, your position started when you began forming in your mother's womb. Your entry into this world was the start of your mission. You had to travel through the journey of life to gather all of the testimonies and trials you needed to fulfill your assignment!" God never intended for me to be broken, defeated, and depressed. He never intended for defeat to take over my life. However, when it did, He made sure I knew about redemption through HIS son Jesus Christ because I had a mission. Jesus didn't just endure the cross to redeem me, but each and every one of us who declares Him as our Lord and Savior (John 3:16).

There was always a higher purpose behind my pain. If the tragic loss of my little girl has taught me anything, it's that LOVE can conquer all of life's hurts, sorrows and pains. God loved me out of darkness and into the light. He drew me with loving kindness and loved me with his everlasting love (Jer. 31:3). He groomed me and made me into the woman I was originally meant to be. I am the apple of His eye, and so are you. I met Jesus when I was at my lowest point in life, and He loved me to my highest. I am strong through Him. I have unspeakable joy because of Him. I have compassion and peace, and it's all because Jesus loved me into it. The Word of God says that "the Lord is close to the brokenhearted and saves those who are crushed in spirit" (Ps.34:18). Who am I? I am Chakesha (Kesha) Shurn. I am a wife to Eric and I am the mother of Adriana, Mariya and Braylon. Ultimately, I am His daughter, who has been made complete through His son's sacrifice (Col. 2:10). He knew the value in me before I could recognize it myself, but He valued me enough to help me see what He sees. I see it now. I believe that I am fearfully and wonderfully made (Ps. 139:14). I know that my God is so meticulous that He knows my thoughts before I think them, my words before I say them, and has numbered each hair on my head (Matt. 10:30). He loves me and I am His.

Chakesha Shurn

Chapter 12
God's Light

After many difficult therapy sessions, one therapist advised us of the dangers of memorializing Adriana in a way that was unhealthy. Ultimately we came up with an idea to release balloons towards heaven, every year on Adriana's birthday and the anniversary of her death. One particular year, April of 2015 to be exact, it was a Sunday. I woke up to get ready for church, and I struggled to fight back the tears as I remembered this was a day that God allowed me to bring a unique little person into this world, but she was no longer with me. My children and I went to church and stopped by the store on the way home to pick up balloons. On the way home, I could hear a small voice gently say, "I'm here." This had become a tradition not only for our little family, but also my parents, my sisters and my best friend. They would also join in and release balloons from different parts of the country. At one point, my dad moved as far as Las Vegas and still released balloons like clockwork.

When we got home, all four of us proceeded to the backyard, the kids each had one balloon, and I held one in each hand. My husband stood behind me with his camera ready to catch pictures of my release. We prayed and asked God for strength and grace for this day, because it was a rough day for our family. What he captured in the photo was confirmation that God does exactly what He says He will do. He was there in a visible way. As my husband stood behind me, he was able to capture a single ray of sunshine shining directly down only upon me as I let the balloons go. God was there just as He promised.

Chakesha Shurn

We release balloons every year on Adriana's birthday and the day she passed... So far I have wanted to cry since I woke up... On my way home from church I could hear God gently say "I'm here"... This is what my hubby captured while I released balloons to my angel... God keeps His promises

Mariya and Braylon have always known who their sister is. We have always had pictures of Adriana around. We make sure to tell them stories about the amusing things their sister would do and say, how loving their sister was, and ways they remind us of her. We've also made it routine to include Adriana in our prayers. There were even days where Mariya and Braylon would get so sad thinking about their sister. One day, Braylon's teacher emailed me after school saying that Braylon was incredibly sad in class, and when she asked what was wrong, he said he missed his sister that died. Although he had never met his sister, he felt a strong connection to her and still does to this day.

Braylon and Mariya

Butterflies are not mentioned in the Bible per se, however, I believe the symbolism of butterflies is depicted in 2nd Corinthians Ch. 5:17, which states, "Therefore, if anyone is in Christ, the new creation has come: The old has gone, the new is here!". Adriana came into this world as my precious baby girl. When she was called to her heavenly home, she became a new creature just as a caterpillar becomes a butterfly, a new creature. Every year when I'm having a particularly emotional day, missing my peanut, I can always spot a butterfly flying unusually close to me. Every year around her birthday and the anniversary of her death, I am bombarded with butterflies. It gives me comfort. It has been said that the presence of butterflies means a loved one is close to you. I believe God sends them as comfort.

Amazingly, as I look back now, I can see where God intervened so many times in my life, but I also don't feel like I heard Him or could feel His presence. As I write and reflect on my journey to freedom, I don't know how I made it out, and how I got to where I am now, without hearing His voice. The Footprints poem by Mary Stevenson, became a significant part of who I am when I initially read it. It describes so eloquently the love of my God. He knew my capabilities and where I was in my life. He knew I was not able to hear Him and how oblivious I was to the things swirling around, and would take place in my life. That's why I love the footprints poem cause I feel like He was literally carrying me!

During the summer of 2017, we took a family vacation to Orlando, Florida for about a week with my youngest sister Nicole, and my niece and nephew. It was a scorching sunny day, and as we waited for everyone to pile out of the hotel room, we decided to let the kids play at the playground. This was about day four and Braylon, who was seven years old at the time, was playing on the monkey bars at the resort we were staying at. While attempting to jump to the second bar, he fell and ran to me crying!

We initially thought that it wasn't as bad as it was, but let me tell you how God used this accident to bring full circle my healing from Adriana's death. We were on vacation and didn't have a car, so we called an Uber. When we got in the car, we asked the gentleman to take us to an urgent care center, which we had already contacted to make sure they had x-ray capabilities. The driver asked what happened, and we told him. He suggested it would be best to take us to the hospital in the event that Braylon's arm was broken, because

they would send us there anyways. We
agreed. After arriving to the hospital
and completing x-rays, we discovered
Braylon had broken his wrist and elbow
and would need surgery to repair them.
We were on vacation! How could this be
happening on vacation? I had already
been praying for healing, but this news
prompted more prayer! My baby had
never had surgery before. He was so
small, and I was worried, I have to
admit. Eric had the same look of worry
on his face as we just stared at our
baby boy lying in a hospital bed. We
embraced each other, cried, and
prayed.

During the ambulance transfer to
the children's hospital, Braylon was in
back having a ball, while I sat in the
front of the ambulance in prayer. Eric
had to meet us at the hospital because
there was only so much room in the
ambulance. We met on the assigned
floor at the same time. It was refreshing
to see my husbands face. We got settled
in his room, because neither one of us
was leaving his side, and the nurses
prepared him for surgery later that

morning. Every person we came into contact with was kind, patient, helpful, and all around loving. They displayed the love of Christ as their natural state. They treated our baby as if he was their own. As we spent time in the hospital, we noticed that biblical scriptures were always around us. Everywhere we turned, there was a scripture that was relevant to our process at the time. The comfort of each scripture was extremely critical for my husband and I because they helped us to make it through to the other side of this ordeal. Every nurse, doctor, and EMT that we came in contact with was fantastic! Because of all of the negative emotions that hospitals brought us, having the reassurance of so many (along with the most significant reassurance from God and His word), meant everything.

When we got confirmation that the surgery was complete and everything went well, it hit me. As we sat in the waiting room, I could clearly reflect on God's comforting hand leading and guiding us through this difficult time. I began to weep and praise God right in the middle of the waiting room. I looked around me, and I knew that many people had no clue of God's power and His love for his children. I had such a sense of peace. God has assured us that He "would never leave or forsake us" (Heb. 13:5) and once again, He kept His promise.

Knowing Christ doesn't make me forget my daughter, or the pain of losing her, knowing Christ makes it easier to remember her. Christ makes it easier to endure, to feel, to love, and to exist in a way that I couldn't fathom before Him.

After thought:

Suicide is prevalent in the United States and across the world. You don't have to battle these thoughts and feelings alone.

If you are having suicidal thoughts or know someone who is, any local church is willing to pray with you. If this is not an option, please call the National Suicide Prevention Lifeline at 1-800-273-8255.

ABOUT THE AUTHOR

Chakesha Shurn is a small town girl with a big heart. She was born and raised in South Bend, Indiana, where she graduated from James Whitcomb Riley High School on the Southeast side of South Bend. She is the oldest of three girls. Chakesha is currently residing in the state of Maryland with her husband, Eric and two children, Mariya and Braylon. She loves to sing, listen to music, and spend quality time with her family.

Made in the USA
Lexington, KY
13 March 2018